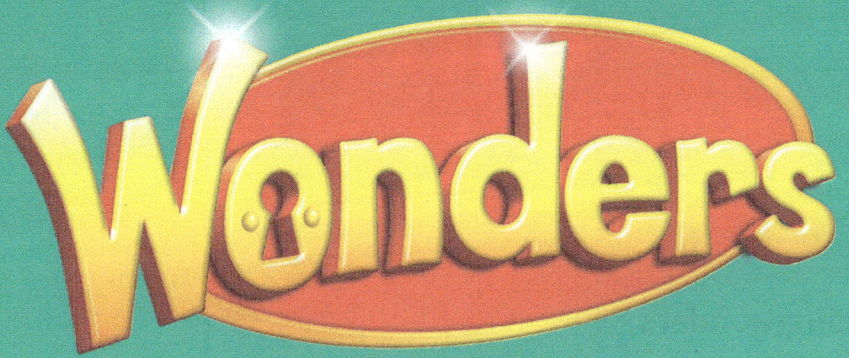

Cover and Title Page: Nathan Love

www.mheonline.com/readingwonders

Copyright © 2017 McGraw-Hill Education

All rights reserved. No part of this publication may be reproduced or distributed in any form or by any means, or stored in a database or retrieval system, without the prior written consent of McGraw-Hill Education, including, but not limited to, network storage or transmission or broadcast for distance learning.

Send all inquiries to:
McGraw-Hill Education
2 Penn Plaza
New York, NY 10121

ISBN: 978-0-02-131383-9
MHID: 0-02-131383-0

Printed in the United States of America.

5 6 7 8 9 10 MER 30 29 28 27 26 25   C

ELD
Companion Worktext

Program Authors

Diane August

Jana Echevarria

Josefina V. Tinajero

Unit 6

Taking Action

The Big Idea
When is it important to take action? 2

Week 1 • Resources 4

More Vocabulary 6
Shared Read The Fortunes of Fragrance Genre • Expository .... 8
Respond to the Text 12
Write to Sources 14

Week 2 • Witnesses 16

More Vocabulary 18
Shared Read The Great Fire of London
  Genre • Narrative Nonfiction 20
Respond to the Text 24
Write to Sources 26

Week 3 • Investigations 28

More Vocabulary 30
Shared Read Researcher to the Rescue Genre • Expository 32
Respond to the Text 36
Write to Sources 38

Week 4 • Extraordinary Finds 40

More Vocabulary 42
Shared Read Messages in Stone and Wood Genre • Expository 44
Respond to the Text 48
Write to Sources 50

Week 5 • Taking a Break 52

More Vocabulary 54
Shared Read "An Ode to the Wind" Genre • Poetry 56
Respond to the Text 58
Write to Sources 60

UNIT 6
Taking Action

The Big Idea

When is it important to take action?

TALK ABOUT IT

Weekly Concept Resources

? Essential Question
How have people used natural resources?

>> *Go Digital*

 What is the man's job? What is the natural resource? How do the man and the bees help each other? Write words in the chart.

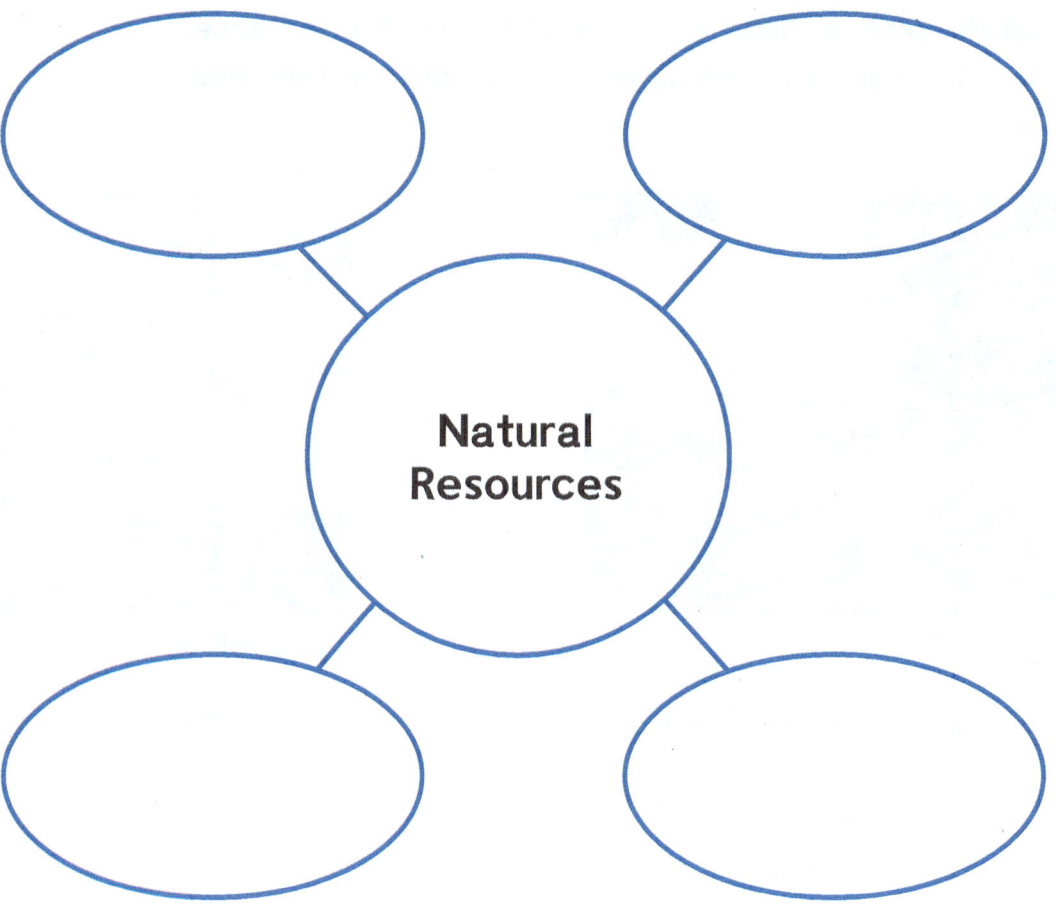

Discuss how the man is using a natural resource. Use words from the chart. Complete the sentences.

The man is taking care of the _____. The man helps

the bees by building _____. The bees _____

crops and make _____ for the man to sell.

More Vocabulary

 Look at the picture. Read the word. Then read the sentence. Talk about the word with a partner. Write your own sentence.

extract

Brett needs to extract the nail from his tire.

What word means the same as *extract*?

give   remove   tell

What can a dentist extract?

A dentist can extract _____

_____

_____

preserve

Freezing food will help preserve it.

Complete the sentence. Write the word.

You _____ something that you want to keep.

What do you want to preserve?

I want to preserve _____

_____

Words and Phrases: Multiple-Meaning Words

The word *scent* means "a smell."

What has a nice scent?

Flowers have a nice **scent**.

The word *scent* can also mean "to fill with a smell."

What will the flowers scent?

The flowers will **scent** the room.

Talk with a partner. Look at the pictures. Read the sentences. Underline the correct meaning of the word *scent*.

This flower has a nice *scent*.

a smell   to fill with a smell

These trees *scent* the air.

a smell   to fill with a smell

Text Evidence

Shared Read | Genre • Expository Text

1 Talk About It

Look at the photographs. Read the title and captions. Discuss what you see. Use these words.

**business   rose blossoms
fragrance   tanks**

Write about what you see.

The text is about _____

_____.

What is the man doing?

He is holding _____

_____.

What things are used to make perfume in France?

_____ are used to make perfume in France.

Take notes as you read the text.

The Fortunes of Fragrance

Essential Question

? How have people used natural resources?

Read about the natural resources used to make fragrances from ancient times to today.

Rose blossoms grown in Morocco

8

Our sense of smell helps us survive. It helps us **detect** poisons, toxic gases, rotten food, and other dangers. For centuries, doctors have used their sense of smell to find infection or disease. Fortunately, there are many pleasant odors, as well. From earliest times, people have looked for ways to **preserve** the lovely scents of flowers and herbs.

Capturing Aromas

Many plants smell good to us. Early humans discovered how to crush leaves, fruits, and bark to release these smells. Before long, they found ways to release the oils and burn parts of plants to scent the air. They soaked rose petals in water to make a scented liquid. They also mixed tree sap with honey to make a lump of incense. They placed the incense on hot coals or burners to make a perfumed smoke.

Over time, people found other ways to capture fragrances from plants. They squeezed the rinds of citrus fruits. They also boiled lavender or peppermint leaves. Later, they found that steam could also be used to **extract** oils from plants. This technique, called *steam distillation*, is still widely used today.

Tanks used to make perfume in France.

Text Evidence

❶ Specific Vocabulary

Read the first paragraph. The word *detect* means "identify." Underline another word in the paragraph that means almost the same thing as *detect*. What does our sense of smell help us detect?

Our sense of smell helps us detect _____ _____.

❷ Sentence Structure

Read the first sentence of the third paragraph. What phrase tells you that learning to capture fragrances happened over many years? Circle the phrase.

❸ Comprehension
Main Idea and Key Details

Read the third paragraph. What are three ways that people captured fragrances from plants? Underline the sentences that tell you.

Text Evidence

1 Talk About It

Read the first paragraph. Why did people use animal fat instead of steam distillation to absorb the fragrance from flowers?

Steam distillation is too _____

_____.

2 Sentence Structure ACT

Read the last sentence in the second paragraph. Underline the independent clause. Circle the dependent clause. What places did the Silk Road trade routes link?

The Silk Road trade routes linked

_____.

3 Comprehension
Main Idea and Key Details

Read "Trading in Aromatics." Why were fragrant plants valuable in the ancient world? Underline two details that tell you.

FLOWERS
Jasmine, Rose

PODS, SEEDS
Vanilla Pod, Anise Seed

BARK
Cinnamon, Birch

LEAVES
Peppermint, Patchouli

ROOTS, RHIZOMES
Vetiver Root, Iris Rhizome

Some flowers cannot stand up to the heat of steam. So people learned to press them into animal fat. The fat absorbs the fragrance. Then the fat is washed in alcohol. After the alcohol evaporates, only the fragrance remains as something called a *concrete*. This process, however, is time-consuming and expensive. Today, chemicals are used to extract fragrances from delicate flowers.

Trading in Aromatics

Most fragrant plants are quite portable, so they became widely traded commodities in the ancient world. If a resource for a scent was very hard to find, it could be more valuable than gold. In the ancient world, myrrh, camphor, cinnamon, sandalwood, and frankincense were carried hundreds of miles by land and by sea. These resources were traded along the Silk Road trade routes, which linked Greece, Rome, Arabia, China, and India.

Then in the Middle Ages, Europeans discovered the perfumes and spices of the Far East. Demand for these scents increased. The Europeans began to look for sea trade routes that went around the dominant merchants in the Middle East.

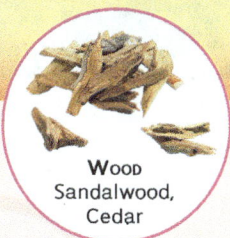 **Wood** Sandalwood, Cedar

 **Berries** Black Pepper, Juniper Berry

 **Citrus Rinds** Lime, Lemon

 **Sap, Resins** Frankincense, Myrrh

The Enduring Power of Perfume

In the modern world, chemists are the new explorers. These scientists have learned to make synthetic replacements for fragrant plant oils. Synthetic, or not natural, perfumes are usually less expensive than perfumes made of natural materials, because the supplies are not affected by weather conditions or crop yields.

But many high-quality perfumes still require ingredients that come from real flowers. One perfume company maintains its own fields in the south of France to grow roses and jasmine flowers for their scents.

Demand for fragrances has only increased since ancient times. The industry is now worth billions of dollars. As long as people seek beautiful aromas, the fragrance market will continue to be big business.

Early perfume bottles were decorated.

Make Connections

 Talk about how the demand for fragrances changed technology and trade. **ESSENTIAL QUESTION**

Describe the scent of a household product you use often. What do you like or dislike about it? **TEXT TO SELF**

Text Evidence

❶ Specific Vocabulary

Read the first paragraph. Circle the phrase that helps you understand the meaning of *synthetic*. Why are synthetic perfumes usually less expensive than perfumes made of natural materials?

Synthetic perfumes _____

_____.

❷ Talk About It

Read the second paragraph. Why does one perfume company keep flower fields in the south of France?

Many high-quality perfumes _____

_____.

❸ Comprehension
Main Idea and Key Details

Reread the last paragraph. The main idea is that demand for fragrances has increased since ancient times. Underline a key detail that supports this idea.

Respond to the Text

 **Partner Discussion** Work with a partner. Read the questions about "The Fortunes of Fragrance." Show where you found text evidence. Write the page numbers. Then discuss what you learned.

How did early humans capture good smells?

Early humans crushed _____.   Page(s): _____

Before long, they soaked _____ and burned _____.   Page(s): _____

What resources and methods did people use over time?

People found ways to capture fragrances from _____.   Page(s): _____

They used a few methods, such as _____

_____.   Page(s): _____

How did interest in capturing aromas affect trade?

Rare resources became _____.   Page(s): _____

So traders traveled along _____ and then to _____.   Page(s): _____

 **Group Discussion** Present your answers to the group. Cite text evidence for your ideas. Listen to and discuss the group's opinions.

Write Work with a partner. Look at your notes about "The Fortunes of Fragrance." Write your answer to the Essential Question. Use text evidence to support your answer. Use vocabulary words in your writing.

How have people used natural resources to make perfume?

Early humans _____.

Before long, people _____.

Over time, they used other ways, such as _____
_____.

People liked fragrances so much that they used rare _____,

such as _____.

To obtain valuable rare resources, traders _____
_____.

Share Writing Present your writing to the class. Discuss their opinions. Talk about their ideas. Explain why you agree or disagree with their ideas. You can say:

I agree with _____.

That's a good comment, but _____.

13

Write to Sources

Mateo

pages 8–11

Take Notes About the Text I took notes on my two-column chart to answer the question: *What can I learn from the text features in "The Fortunes of Fragrance"?*

Text Feature	What I Learned
1. Photo--Rose blossoms grown in Morocco	1. Many flowers are needed to make perfume.
2. Photo--Copper tanks	2. Large, copper tanks can be used to make perfume.
3. Illustrations--Types of flowers and plants	3. Many types of flowers and plants can be used to make fragrances.
4. Photo--Fancy perfume bottles	4. Perfume was kept in fancy bottles because it was very important.

Write About the Text I used notes from my chart to write a paragraph about what I learned from the text features in the text.

Student Model: *Informative Text*

The text features in "The Fortunes of Fragrance" help me learn how fragrances are made. The photo of the field of roses shows that many flowers are needed to make perfume. The photo of the large, copper tanks shows how some fragrances are made. The illustrations show many types of flowers and plants. These flowers and plants are used to make many different fragrances. Finally, the fancy perfume bottles show that perfume was very important. These photos and illustrations all help me learn how fragrances are made.

TALK ABOUT IT

Text Evidence
Draw a box around a sentence that comes from the notes about equipment for making perfume. Why did Mateo use this detail?

Grammar
Circle the two adjectives in the third sentence. What is the function of these adjectives?

Condense Ideas
Underline two sentences about flowers and plants shown in the illustrations. How can you use the word *that* to condense the ideas?

Your Turn

How were perfumes made in the past? How are they made today? Tell how the processes are alike and different.

>> *Go Digital!*
Write your response online. Use your editing checklist.

TALK ABOUT IT

Weekly Concept Witnesses

? Essential Question
How do we learn about historical events?

>> *Go Digital*

 What is the man in the photo wearing? Who is he pretending to be? How is he helping the boy learn about history? Write words in the chart.

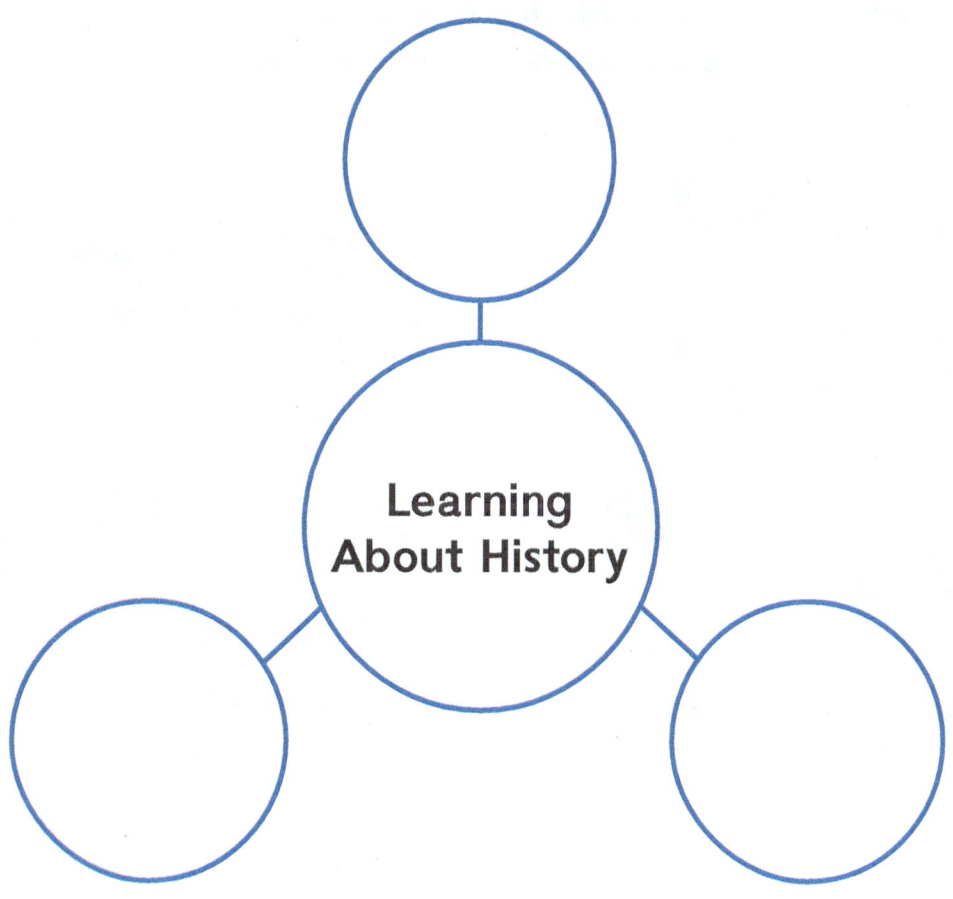

Discuss how the man is helping the boy learn about history. Use words from the chart. Complete these sentences.

The man is wearing a _____ and _____. He is

dressed like a _____. He is teaching the boy about

soldiers during _____.

More Vocabulary

 Look at the picture. Read the word. Then read the sentence. Talk about the word with a partner. Write your own sentence.

accidental

Sam's fall from his bike was **accidental**.

Complete the sentence. Write the word.

Something _____ is not planned.

Name something that was accidental.

_____ was accidental.

recorded

Adrian **recorded** the main points of the teacher's story.

What word means the same thing as *recorded*?

wrote   listened   read

What have you recorded this week?

This week, I recorded _____

_____.

Words and Phrases: Compound Words

The word *storeroom* means "a room where things are stored, or kept."

Where does the factory keep the food?

It keeps the food in a **storeroom**.

The word *watchmaker* means "a person who makes watches."

What is this man's job?

This man is a **watchmaker**.

Talk with a partner. Look at the pictures. Read the sentences. Underline the word that completes the sentence.

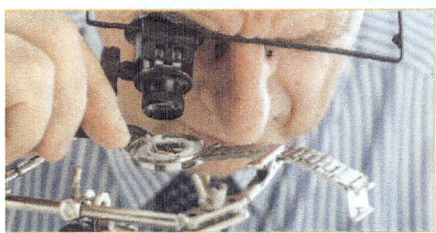

This person is a _____.

watcher   watchmaker   maker

These things are stored in a _____.

storeroom   story   storm

Text Evidence

Shared Read | Genre • Narrative Nonfiction

1 Talk About It

Look at the illustration. Read the title. Discuss what you see. Use these words.

buildings	carts
wheeling	burning

Write about what you see.

What does the title tell you?

The text is about _____

_____.

What does the illustration show you?

The illustration shows _____

_____.

It also shows people _____

_____.

Take notes as you read the text.

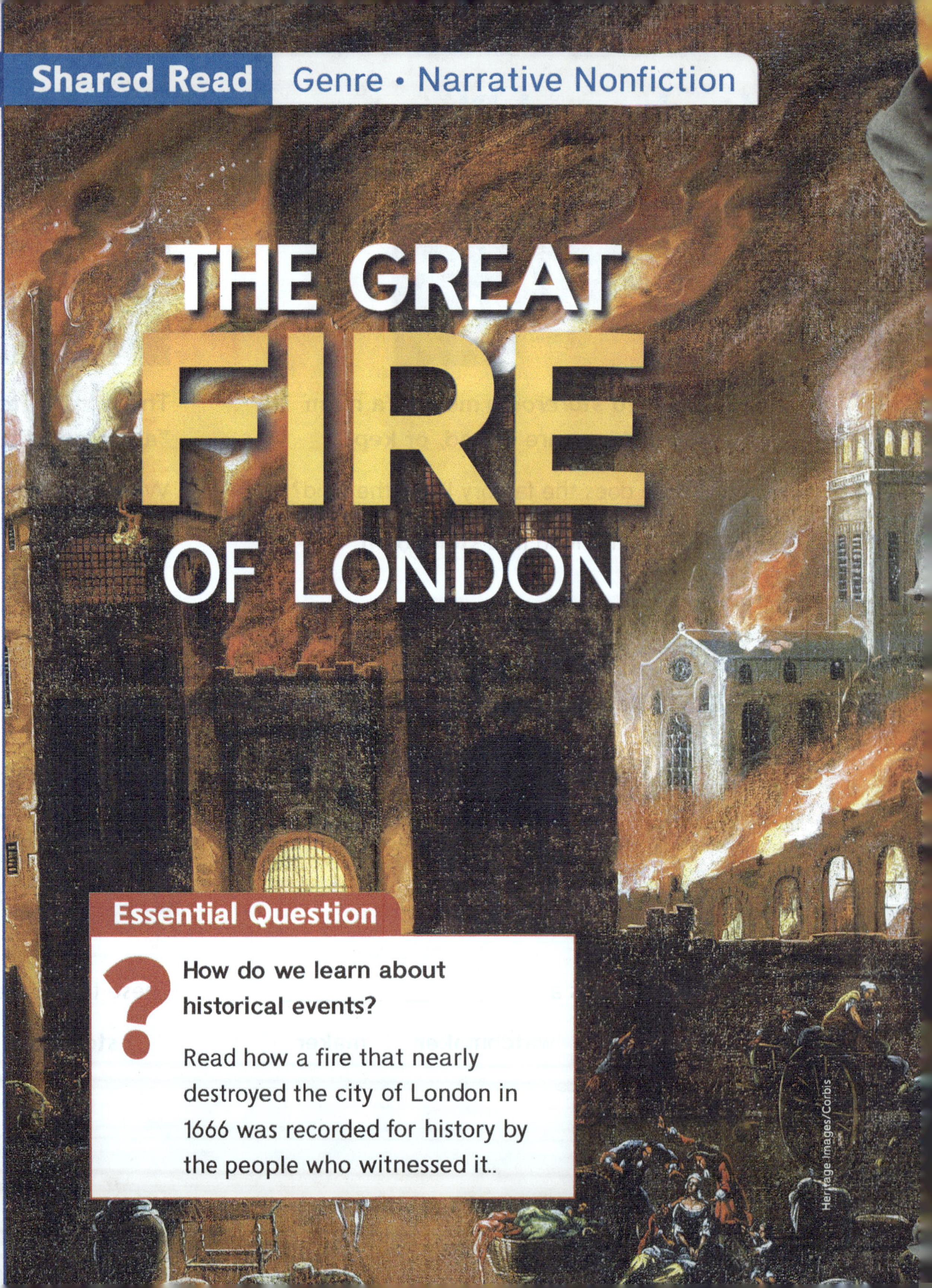

THE GREAT FIRE OF LONDON

Essential Question

? How do we learn about historical events?

Read how a fire that nearly destroyed the city of London in 1666 was recorded for history by the people who witnessed it..

London in 1666

In 1666, London was the most populous city in Europe. And it was growing fast. Nearly 500,000 people crowded into its old wooden buildings. Storerooms were filled with flammable goods, such as oil and tallow. Open fires burned in hearths day and night.

Accidental fires were common. Some people feared that fire would destroy London someday. Others were more worried about the plague, a sickness that had killed nearly 68,000 people. The summer of 1666 had been unusually hot and dry. A single spark was all that was needed to cause disaster.

A seventeenth-century painting shows the Great Fire of London.

Fire Breaks Out

The spark occurred early in the morning on September 2, 1666. Officially, the fire started at the King's Bakery on Pudding Street. Samuel Pepys, an administrator living in London, **recorded** his observations in a diary. He wrote that the baker's family woke up choking on smoke. A strong wind then fanned the flames, sending sparks to ignite other buildings. Fire quickly spread to surrounding streets.

Text Evidence

❶ Specific Vocabulary

Read the third sentence. The word *flammable* means "easy to set on fire." Circle two examples of flammable items. Where were the flammable goods?

The flammable goods were in

_____.

❷ Sentence Structure

Read the third sentence in the second paragraph. What is the name of the sickness that had killed nearly 68,000 people? Circle the noun phrase that tells you.

❸ Comprehension
Cause and Effect

Read the last paragraph. What were two effects of the wind fanning the flames?

Sparks ignited _____

_____.

Flames quickly _____

_____.

Text Evidence

1. Talk About It

Read the first paragraph. How did people fight fires in 1666? Write your ideas.

People _____.

They also _____.

2. Comprehension
Cause and Effect

Read the third paragraph. What event caused molten metal to "run down the streets in a stream"? Underline the words that tell you.

3. Specific Vocabulary

Reread the third sentence in the third paragraph. Circle the context clues that help you understand the meaning of *molten*. Then write the meaning of the word.

Molten means _____.

St. Paul's Cathedral in flames (above); a fire syringe used to spray water (left)

In the 1600s, London had no fire department. People threw water on the fire from leather buckets. They beat the flames with brooms. But it was "too little too late." Pepys watched as the "lamentable fire" reached the River Thames, burning warehouses and half of London Bridge. Desperate to save their lives and belongings from the flames, people leaped into boats to escape. Others pulled carts to save the few belongings they could.

London Is Burning

The Lord Mayor led several unsuccessful efforts to stop the fire. He said the fire "overtakes us faster than we can do it." Sparks even ignited the rubble from torn-down houses. As flames spread in new directions, panic spread through the city.

John Evelyn, a well-known writer, described fighting the flames. The ground under his feet was so hot, he noted, that it "even burnt the soles of my shoes." When the fire reached St. Paul's Cathedral, the heat melted the lead roof, causing molten metal to "run down the streets in a stream" and stones from the walls to explode outward.

The fire raged for four days. The *London Gazette* reported that "all attempts for quenching it . . . seemed insufficient." Finally, crucial relief came when the fire reached a brick wall near a law school and the winds changed direction. By that time, most of the city had become a smoldering ruin. Thousands of London's residents were homeless.

The City Builds Again

After the fire, people wanted someone to blame. A French watchmaker named Robert Hubert said he had set the fire. Few people believed him, but he was still hanged. By 1667, Parliament had formally declared the fire an accident, saying it was nothing "other than . . . a great wind, and the season so very dry."

Where there is life there is hope, and people began to rebuild. Many of the new buildings were constructed of stone to protect against fire. The fire also halted the devastation of the plague. It had destroyed the city's rats and their plague-infested fleas.

Make Connections

Talk about ways in which personal and official records help us understand what happened during London's Great Fire. **ESSENTIAL QUESTION**

Describe an event that you and others witnessed. Tell what each of your accounts added to the overall understanding of the event. **TEXT TO SELF**

Text Evidence

1 Sentence Structure

Read the first paragraph. Circle the phrase *by that time*. By what time was the city a smoldering ruin? Draw a box around the words that tell you.

2 Comprehension
Cause and Effect

Read the last paragraph. What were two important effects of the Great Fire of London? Underline the sentences that tell you.

3 Specific Vocabulary

Reread the last sentence of the last paragraph. The word *infested* means "full of something." The compound word *plague-infested* means "full of the plague." What destroyed the city's rats and their plague-infested fleas?

_____

destroyed the city's rats and their plague-infested fleas.

Respond to the Text

 **Partner Discussion** Work with a partner. Read the questions about "The Great Fire of London." Show where you found text evidence. Write the page numbers. Then discuss what you learned.

What do we learn from the author about the Great Fire?

At the beginning, we learn that the fire occurred on _____.

At the end, we learn that the fire destroyed _____.

Text Evidence

Page(s): _____

Page(s): _____

What do we learn about the Fire from people who were there?

Samuel Pepys kept a diary. He watched as _____.

John Evelyn fought the fire. He wrote about _____.

Text Evidence

Page(s): _____

Page(s): _____

What do we learn about the Great Fire from historical records?

The *London Gazette* reported that "_____."

Parliament declared that the fire had been _____.

Text Evidence

Page(s): _____

Page(s): _____

 **Group Discussion** Present your answers to the group. Cite text evidence for your ideas. Listen to and discuss the group's opinions.

 **Write** Work with a partner. Look at your notes about "The Great Fire of London." Write your answer to the Essential Question. Use text evidence to support your answer. Use vocabulary words in your writing.

How do we learn about historical events, such as the Great Fire of London?

We learn about historical events from information an author shares. For example, _____

_____.

We learn from people who were there. For example, _____

_____

_____.

We learn from historical records. For example, _____

_____

_____.

Share Writing Present your writing to the class. Discuss their opinions. Talk about their ideas. Explain why you agree or disagree with their ideas. You can say:

I agree with _____.

That's a good comment, but _____.

Write to Sources

Take Notes About the Text I took notes on a two-column chart to answer the question: *Which disaster was worse--the plague or the Great Fire of London?*

pages 20–23

The Plague	The Great Fire of London
1. The plague killed nearly 68,000 people.	1. The Great Fire left thousands of people homeless.
2. London's rats and their plague-infested fleas spread the plague.	2. The Great Fire destroyed most of London in four days.
3. The Great Fire stopped the plague. It killed the rats and their plague-infested fleas.	3. London was rebuilt after the fire. The new buildings were made of stone. Stone is safer than wood.

Write About the Text I used my notes from my chart to write an argument that explains why the plague was worse than the Great Fire of London.

Student Model: *Argument*

The Great Fire of London was devastating. It destroyed most of London in four days. Thousands of people were left homeless. However, the plague was even worse. Nearly 68,000 people died of the plague. Also, some good things happened after the Great Fire. London was rebuilt. The new buildings were safer. They were made of stone. Also, the Great Fire stopped the plague. It killed the rats and their plague-infested fleas, which spread the plague. The plague was worse than the Great Fire because it killed more people and had no good effects.

TALK ABOUT IT

Text Evidence
Circle the sentence that comes from the notes and tells how the plague was spread. Why did Gabrielle include this information in her writing?

Grammar
Draw a box around the verbs in the first four sentences. What tense are these verbs? Why?

Connect Ideas
Underline sentences 8 and 9. How can you use the word *because* to combine the sentences to connect ideas?

Your Turn

How could London have prevented the Great Fire? Or would the fire have happened eventually? Explain.

>> *Go Digital!*
Write your response online. Use your editing checklist.

TALK ABOUT IT

Weekly Concept Investigations

? **Essential Question**
How can a scientific investigation be an adventure?

>> *Go Digital*

 Where is the scientist in the photo working? What is he doing? Why is his work an adventure? Write words in the chart.

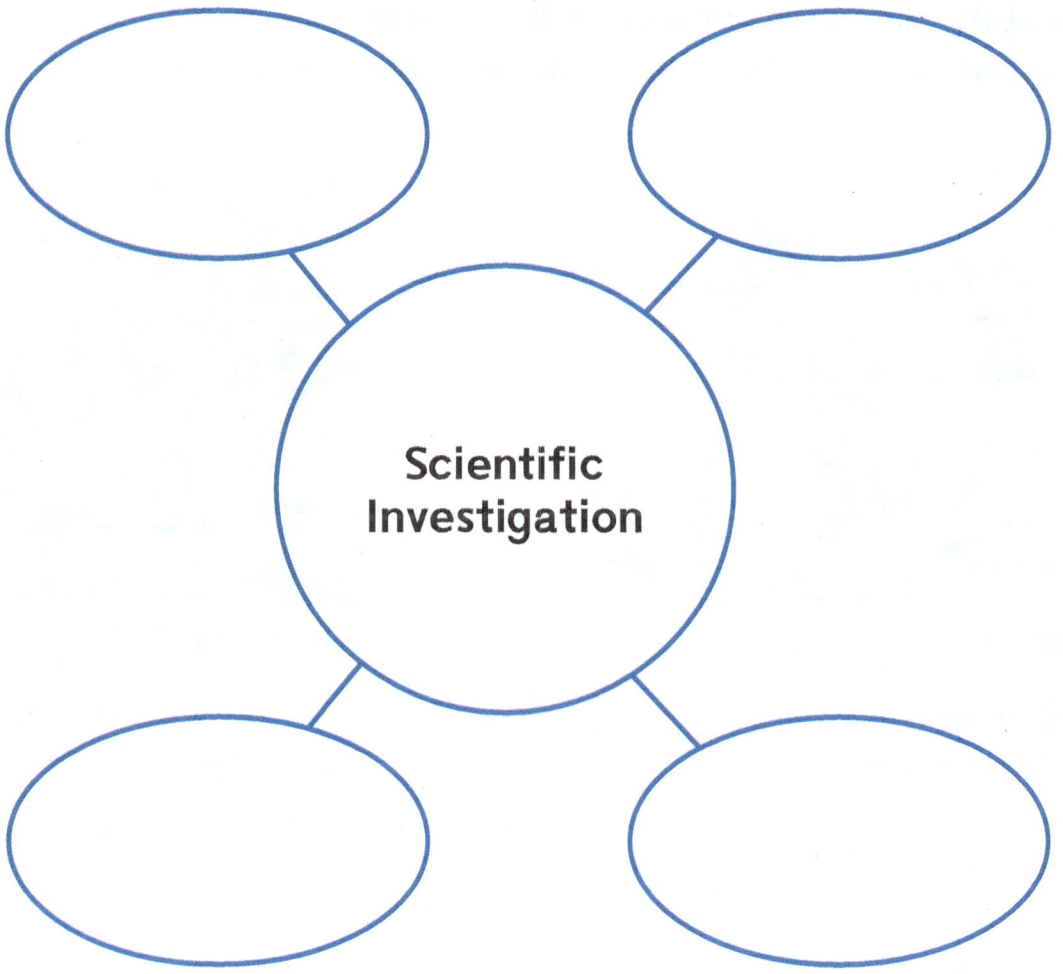

Discuss why the scientist's investigation is an adventure. Use words from the chart. You can say:

The scientist is studying _____. They are in a _____.

It is _____ underground and _____.

More Vocabulary

 Look at the picture. Read the word. Then read the sentence. Talk about the word with a partner. Write your own sentence.

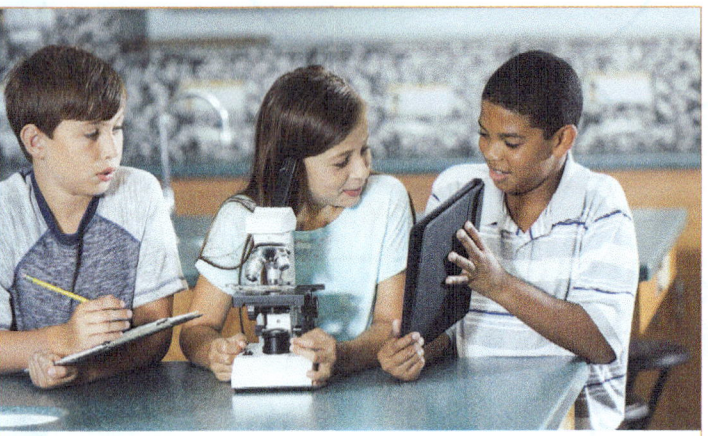

collaboration

The **collaboration** between Isaiah, Deb, and Justin helped them win a prize.

What phrase means the same thing as *collaboration*?

working alone   working together
not working

What kind of **collaboration** have you been in?

I was in a collaboration with _____, and we _____.

investigation

The students are doing a scientific **investigation**.

Complete the sentence. Write the word.

An _____ usually includes research.

What **investigation** do you know about?

I know about a scientific investigation to _____.

Words and Phrases: Multiple-Meaning Words

The word *watch* means "something that gives the time."

What time is it?

This **watch** shows that it is six o'clock.

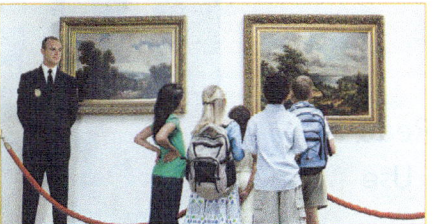

The word *watch* also means "to guard or protect."

What will the security guard do?

He will **watch** the paintings.

 Talk with a partner. Look at the pictures. Read the sentences. Circle the correct meaning of the word *watch*.

Emi loves her new watch.

something that gives the time

to guard or protect

The sailor will watch his ship.

something that gives the time

to guard or protect

Text Evidence

Shared Read | Genre • Expository Text

1 Talk About It

Look at the photographs. Read the title. Discuss what you see. Use these words.

researcher   water   rescue

sea animal   manatee

Write about what you see.

This text is about _____

_____.

Where is the man?

The man is in the _____

_____.

What is the man doing?

The man is holding a _____

_____.

Take notes as you read the text.

RESEARCHER TO THE RESCUE

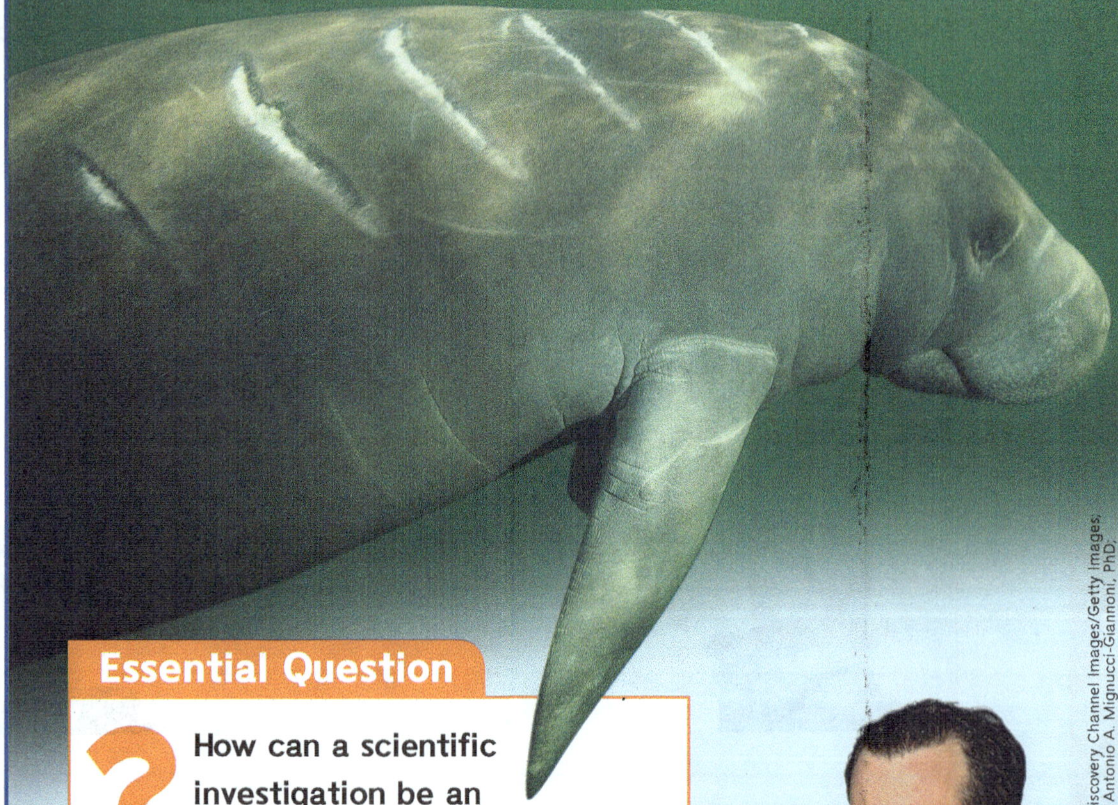

Essential Question

How can a scientific investigation be an adventure?

Read about a biologist's work to protect sea animals.

Manatee Rescue

Dr. Antonio Mignucci is in Florida to keep watch as crew members lift an 840-pound manatee onto a National Guard plane. Today's team of scientists and military personnel form a unique **collaboration**. They teamed up to save the life of a six-year-old manatee that was wounded when a boat struck him.

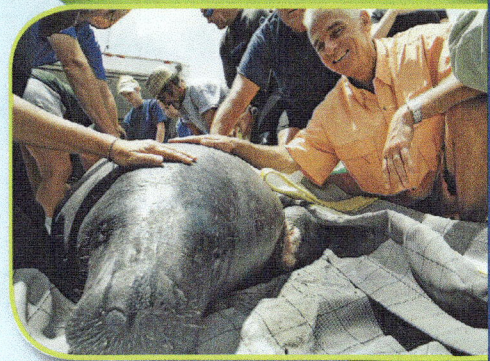

Transporting a manatee

The team transports the manatee to the Puerto Rico Manatee Conservation Center. Dr. Mignucci names the manatee Guacara, after the river where the animal was stranded. Guacara will act as surrogate parent to younger manatees recovering at the Center.

Unlike some marine mammals, manatees cannot stay **submerged**, or under water, for long periods of time. So manatees live in shallow water. But these coastal waters are crowded with boats that could injure and even kill the slow-moving creatures.

Manatees are naturally resilient, but they sometimes need help to recover from injuries. As a marine biologist, Dr. Mignucci recognizes when it's time to extract manatees from tough situations. Guacara's injuries make him "negatively buoyant." In other words, Guacara sinks in deep water. But he can swim safely in shallow pools at the Center.

Text Evidence

❶ Sentence Structure

Read the first sentence. The word *as* tells you that two events happen at the same time. Circle the word *as*. Underline the two events that happen at the same time.

❷ Specific Vocabulary

Read the first sentence in the third paragraph. Circle the context clue that helps you understand the meaning of *submerged*. Since manatees cannot stay submerged for long periods of time, where do they live?

They live in _____.

❸ Comprehension
Main Idea and Details

Read the fourth paragraph. The main idea is that manatees sometimes need people to help them recover from injuries. Underline a detail that supports this main idea.

Text Evidence

1 Specific Vocabulary

Read the first paragraph. Circle the word *extinct*. Underline the context clues that help you understand the meaning of *extinct*.

Extinct means "_____."

2 Comprehension
Main Idea and Details

Read the first and second paragraphs. The main idea is that working together is important. Underline two examples of researchers working together.

3 Talk About It

Reread the second paragraph. Why is it difficult to get an accurate body temperature measurement of a manatee?

Getting a manatee's temperature is difficult. Manatees _____

_____

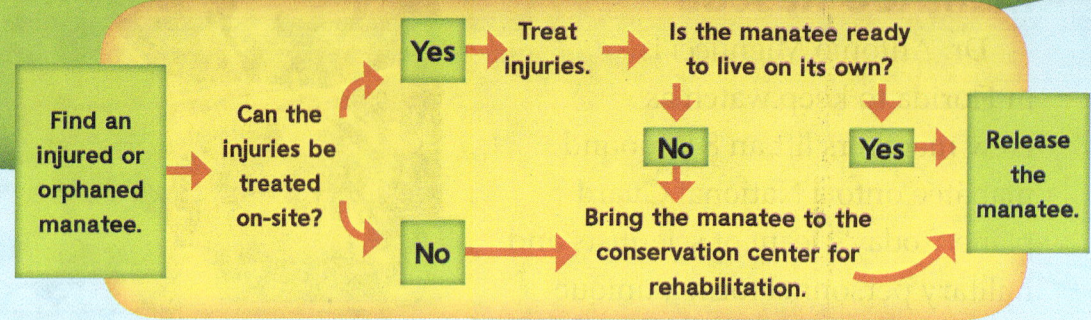

Working Together

Dr. Mignucci investigates a wide variety of marine animals. He considers collaboration to be an important part of research. Dr. Mignucci worked with the Seal Conservation Society of the United Kingdom to find out whether the Caribbean monk seal is extinct. Several sightings suggested that a few of the seals might still be alive. In the end, however, the investigation concluded that the Caribbean monk seal truly is extinct.

Collaboration has also helped Dr. Mignucci solve some unusual problems. Veterinarians at the Center need to get accurate body temperature measurements. Manatees chew anything you put in their mouths, so oral thermometers don't work. Dr. Mignucci got help from a company that makes animal tracking devices. The company provided microchips about the size of a grain of rice. Once a chip is implanted, it can be scanned to find the manatee's body temperature.

To help manatees, Dr. Mignucci has even ventured into the recording studio. Dr. Mignucci collaborated with musician Tony Croatto, who was well known for his versions of Puerto Rican folk songs.

Singing for Support

Croatto and Mignucci cowrote a song called "Moisés llegó del mar" ("Moses Came from the Sea"). Moisés is the name of the first manatee Dr. Mignucci rescued. Moisés was separated from his mother when he was just two weeks old. After 27 months of care, Dr. Mignucci and his team released a healthy Moisés back into the Caribbean. Moisés was the first captive-raised manatee to be rehabilitated and released.

Moisés's song was played around the world and was admired by many listeners. Today, Moisés lives in the wild, where the Center's staff regularly watch his progress.

Dr. Antonio Mignucci at work

Make Connections

Talk about how the doctors work together to help marine animals. **ESSENTIAL QUESTION**

Describe how you could work with others to research and help a local species. **TEXT TO SELF**

Text Evidence

❶ Sentence Structure

Read the second sentence. Circle the comma. Box the dependent clause. What was Tony Croatto well known for?

Tony Croatto was well known for

_____.

❷ Comprehension
Main Idea and Details

Read the second paragraph. The main idea is that Moisés was the first manatee to be rehabilitated and released. Circle two details that support this main idea.

❸ Talk About It

Read the second and third paragraphs. How can a song about Moisés help save other manatees?

The song helps people understand

that _____

_____.

Respond to the Text

 **Partner Discussion** Work with a partner. Read the questions about "Researcher to the Rescue." Show where you found text evidence. Write the page numbers. Then discuss what you learned.

What excitement has Dr. Mignucci had as a marine biologist? Dr. Mignucci, scientists, and military personnel teamed up to _____. Dr. Mignucci watched as crew members _____.	**Text Evidence** Page(s): _____ Page(s): _____

What discoveries and ventures has Dr. Mignucci been a part of? Dr. Mignucci worked with seal experts. Together, they discovered that the Caribbean monk seal _____. Dr. Mignucci helped to solve problems. He used a microchip to _____. Dr. Mignucci ventured into a recording studio. He cowrote _____.	**Text Evidence** Page(s): _____ Page(s): _____ Page(s): _____

 **Group Discussion** Present your answers to the group. Cite text evidence for your ideas. Listen to and discuss the group's opinions.

Write Work with a partner. Look at your notes about "Researcher to the Rescue." Write your answer to the Essential Question. Use text evidence to support your answer. Use vocabulary words in your writing.

How have Dr. Mignucci's scientific investigations been adventures?

Dr. Mignucci's scientific investigations have been exciting. He has watched _____

_____.

Dr. Mignucci has made exciting discoveries during his investigations. He has discovered that _____

_____.

Dr. Mignucci has collaborated on a song about _____

_____.

Share Writing Present your writing to the class. Discuss their opinions. Talk about their ideas. Explain why you agree or disagree with their ideas. You can say:

I agree with _____.

That's a good comment, but _____.

Write to Sources

Sarah

Take Notes About the Text I took notes on an idea web to answer the question: *Why did Dr. Mignucci cowrite a song about a manatee?*

pages 32–35

Detail
Moisés was separated from his mother when he was two weeks old.

Detail
Dr. Mignucci rescued Moisés.

Topic
Song about Moisés

Detail
Dr. Mignucci and his team cared for Moisés and then released him back into the Caribbean.

Detail
Dr. Mignucci cowrote a song about Moisés. The song was played and admired.

38

Write About the Text I used notes from my idea web to write an informative text about the song about Moisés.

Student Model: *Informative Text*

Dr. Mignucci cowrote a song about Moisés. He wanted to raise awareness of Moisés's situation. Moisés was a baby manatee. He was separated from his mother when he was two weeks old. Dr. Mignucci rescued Moisés. Dr. Mignucci and his team cared for Moisés for 27 months. Then they released him back into the Caribbean. Dr. Mignucci later cowrote a song called "Moses Came From the Sea." The song was played around the world. Many people learned about Moisés. Dr. Mignucci's song made Moisés famous. It made people aware of Moisés's situation and the situation of other sea animals.

TALK ABOUT IT

Text Evidence
Circle background information about Moisés that comes from the notes. Why did Sarah include this information?

Grammar
Draw a box around the pronoun in the second sentence. Whom does this pronoun refer to?

Connect Ideas
Underline sentences 9 and 10. How can you use the word *so* to combine the sentences to connect the ideas?

Your Turn
In what ways did Dr. Mignucci collaborate with others? Give examples.

>> *Go Digital!*
Write your response online. Use your editing checklist.

TALK ABOUT IT

Weekly Concept Extraordinary Finds

? Essential Question
What can scientists reveal about ancient civilizations?

>> Go Digital

 What do you see in the photo? What do some of the figures carry? When and why were they made? Write words and phrases in the chart.

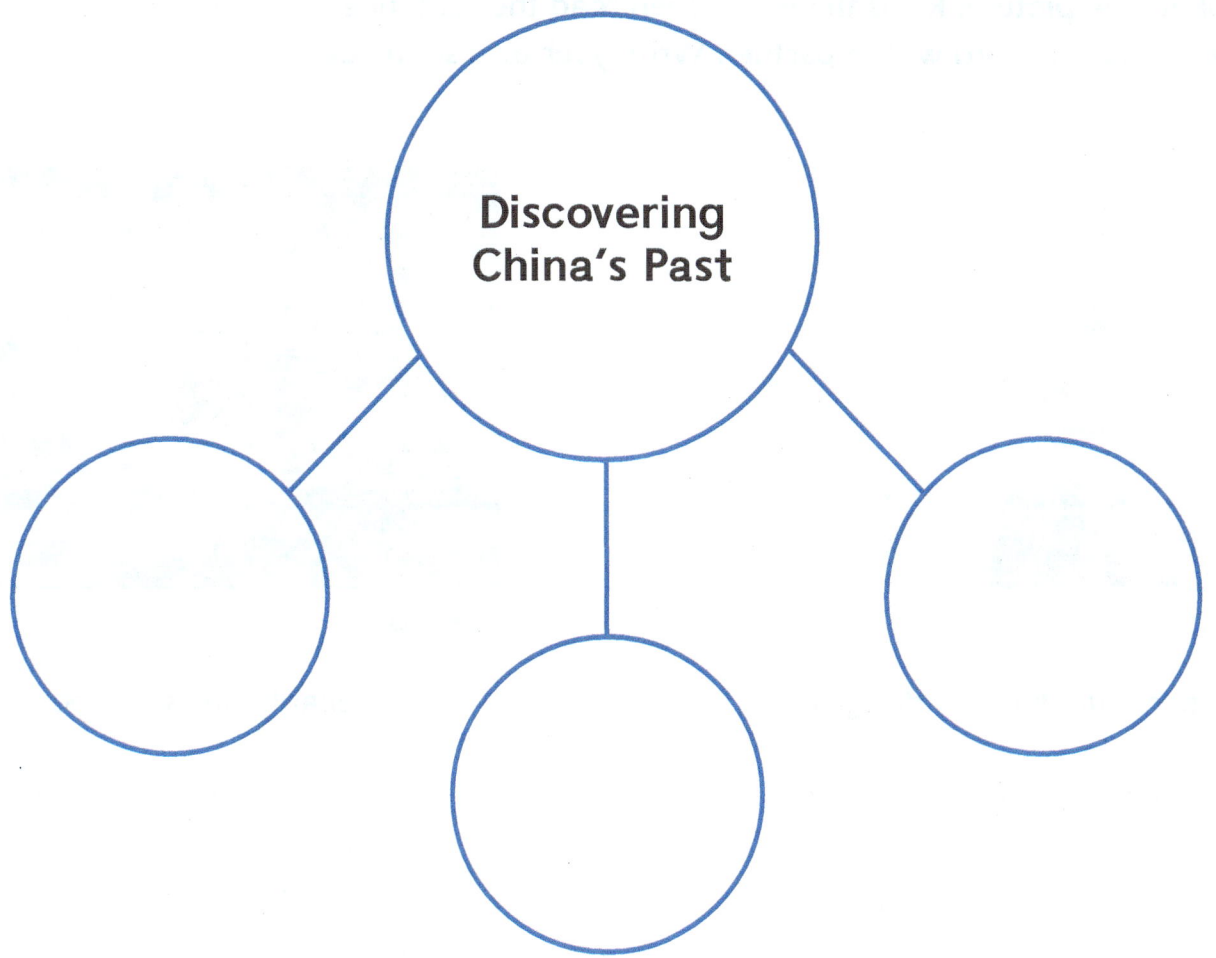

Discuss what scientists found in the tomb of China's first emperor. Use words from the chart. You can say:

The scientists found clay _____. Some carried real _____.

Scientists learned about China more than _____.

More Vocabulary

 Look at the picture. Read the word. Then read the sentence. Talk about the word with a partner. Write your own sentence.

designs

The girls likes to create different **designs**.

What word means the same thing as *designs*?

music   poems   patterns

What kinds of designs do you like?

I like designs that _____
_____.

reliably

Robert **reliably** walks his dog every morning.

Complete the sentence. Write the word.

If you do a job _____, people can depend on you.

What can you do reliably?

I can _____ reliably.

Words and Phrases: *shook* and *shook out*

The word *shook* means "moved something up and down or back and forth."

What did Elena shake?

Elena **shook** Yin's hand.

The phrase *shook out* means "shook so that something came out."

What did Erin shake out of her boot?

Erin **shook out** water.

Talk with a partner. Look at the pictures. Read the sentences. Write the phrase that completes the sentence.

Jordynn _____ salt from the salt shaker.

      shook   **shook out**

Ana _____ the maracas to make music.

      shook   **shook out**

Text Evidence

Shared Read | Genre • Expository Text

1 Talk About It

Look at the photographs. Read the title and captions. Discuss what you see. Use these words.

messages   pictures   stone   wood

Native Americans

Write about what you see.

This text is about _____

_____.

What does the illustration show?

The illustration shows _____

made by _____.

Take notes as you read the text.

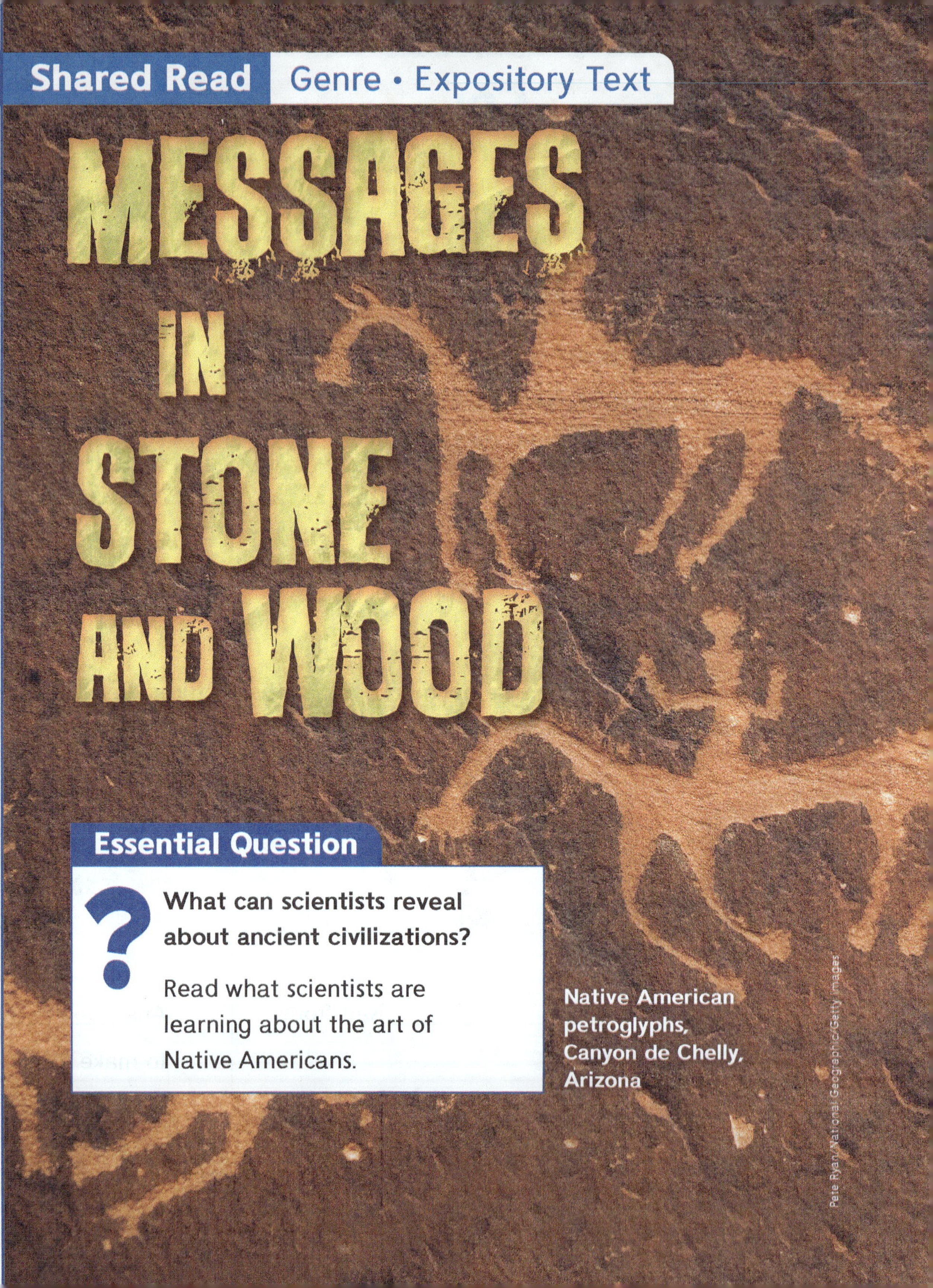

MESSAGES IN STONE AND WOOD

Essential Question

? What can scientists reveal about ancient civilizations?

Read what scientists are learning about the art of Native Americans.

Native American petroglyphs, Canyon de Chelly, Arizona

"We Were Here"

Deep in a forest, members of a hunting party were preparing to embark on their trip home. First, they created a chronicle of their successful hunt. One of the hunters selected a large oak tree. He used a knife to peel back the bark. From a small leather bag, he shook out some powder made from red pebbles. Then he mixed the powder with animal fat to make a thick red paint.

On the tree, the hunter painted images of a turtle and six men carrying packs and bows. He added the heads of three deer and a bear. From then on, anyone passing this spot would see from these **designs** that six men of the terrapin clan had hunted here.

Mysterious Markings

The first Europeans to explore North America came across many markings like the one on the tree. At first, no one understood the meanings of these *petroglyphs* (stone carvings) and *dendroglyphs* (tree carvings and paintings). People studying the markings, or pictographs, learned that Native Americans had made them. The pictographs recorded hunts, battles, and clan meetings.

When non-native people moved farther west during the 1800s, they discovered many more markings. In the dry desert of the Southwest, pictographs on rocks and cave walls appeared to be

Petroglyph of a "Water Panther," Parkers Landing, Pennsylvania

Text Evidence

1 Comprehension
Sequence

Read the first and second paragraphs. What did the hunter do after he made a thick red paint? Underline the sentences that tell you.

2 Specific Vocabulary

Read the third paragraph. Circle a word that means the same thing as *pictographs*. What did the pictographs show?

The pictographs showed

_____.

3 Sentence Structure

Read the first sentence of the fourth paragraph. Circle the comma. Underline the independent clause. Box the dependent clause. What did non-native people discover when they moved farther west in the 1800s?

They discovered _____.

45

Text Evidence

1 Talk About It

Read the first two full sentences. How did weather affect pictographs in the East?

Pictographs in the East were affected by _____.

2 Sentence Structure

Read the first full paragraph. Underline the pronoun *they* in the second sentence. Who could not reliably date the pictographs or agree on their meanings? Circle the noun in the first sentence that the pronoun *they* refers to.

3 Comprehension
Sequence

Reread the first full paragraph. After technology improved, what did scientists learn about some of the rock images? Underline the sentence that tells you.

COMMON PETROGLYPH TYPES

human figures — hand — dog
sheep — elk or deer — fish — bird
snake — spiral — half moon — full moon

freshly made. But in the East, moisture rots dead tree trunks, and ice damages rocks. The only remaining records of many pictographs are copies drawn by early explorers and historians.

Reading the Messages

For a long time, archaeologists made little progress in studying the markings of Native Americans. They could not reliably date the pictographs or agree on their meanings. But technology improved and helped scientists learn more about these images. Scientists learned that some rock images are nearly a thousand years old.

Scientists are better able to determine when markings were made. But understanding their meanings is still difficult. It is generally accepted that the people who made pictographs in open areas wanted to mark borders or record important events. Understanding images hidden in sheltered areas or caves is more challenging.

Archaeologist Rex Weeks, an Echota Cherokee from Alabama, brings an intrinsic cultural perspective to the study of Native American rock images. Dr. Weeks suggests that Native Americans made some images in secluded areas to keep them private. The images were used for ceremonies or to teach young people the beliefs and history of their clan. Many symbols used in images link the cultures of ancient peoples to the Native Americans of today.

Saving Pictographs

Today, many pictographs are in danger of being destroyed by natural forces before they can be documented and studied. Others are damaged when careless excavation by non-professionals ruins them or leaves them exposed to the elements. So experts have developed a system called the Rock Art Stability Index. This index is used to assess which sites are most at risk. Educating the public about the importance of these sites is critical in saving these cultural resources for future generations.

Dr. Rex Weeks

Make Connections

Talk about what archaeologists have learned from the pictographs of early Native Americans. **ESSENTIAL QUESTION**

Compare pictographs to the methods you use today to deliver messages and record events in your life. **TEXT TO SELF**

Text Evidence

❶ Specific Vocabulary

Read the sentence starting at the bottom of page 46. Circle the word that helps you understand the meaning of *secluded*. What were the images used for?

They were used for _____

or to _____.

❷ Sentence Structure

Read the first sentence of the first full paragraph. What needs to happen before many pictographs are destroyed by natural forces?

Before pictographs are destroyed, they need to be _____.

❸ Talk About It

Why is it important to educate the public about the importance of the sites?

It is important that the public does not _____ the sites.

Respond to the Text

 **Partner Discussion** Work with a partner. Read the questions about "Messages in Stone and Wood." Show where you found text evidence. Write the page numbers. Then discuss what you learned.

How has science helped in dating Native American art?

For a long time, scientists could not reliably _____.

But _____ improved, and now scientists can determine _____.

Text Evidence

Page(s): _____

Page(s): _____

What has Dr. Weeks learned by studying pictographs?

Dr. Weeks says the rock images were used for _____.

These images were also used to teach _____

_____.

Text Evidence

Page(s): _____

Page(s): _____

 **Group Discussion** Present your answers to the group. Cite text evidence for your ideas. Listen to and discuss the group's opinions.

 **Write** Work with a partner. Look at your notes about "Messages in Stone and Wood." Write your answer to the Essential Question. Use text evidence to support your answer. Use vocabulary words in your writing.

What have scientists learned about Native Americans from their art?

Scientists have learned that some rock images are _____

_____.

From Native American pictographs, scientists have learned about _____

_____.

The symbols in the pictographs link ancient peoples to _____

_____.

Share Writing Present your writing to the class. Discuss their opinions. Talk about their ideas. Explain why you agree or disagree with their ideas. You can say:

I agree with _____.

That's a good comment, but _____.

Write to Sources

Take Notes About the Text I took notes on the sequence chart to answer the question: *How has our understanding of Native American pictographs changed?*

pages 44–47

First
The first European explorers did not understand the pictographs.

Next
People studied the pictographs. They learned that Native Americans had made them. The pictographs told of hunts and battles. The pictographs told of clan meetings.

Then
Technology improved. Scientists learned that some pictographs were nearly a thousand years old.

Last
An archaelogist named Dr. Weeks suggests that the symbols in some pictographs link the cultures of ancient peoples to Native Americans today.

Write About the Text I used notes from my sequence chart to write an informative text about Native American pictographs.

Student Model: *Informative Text*

Our understanding of Native American pictographs has changed. The first European explorers did not understand the pictographs. Then people studied the markings. They learned that the pictographs told stories of hunts and battles. They also told stories of clan meetings. After technology improved, scientists discovered that some pictographs were nearly a thousand years old. Recently, an archaeologist named Dr. Weeks suggested that the symbols in the pictographs link the cultures of ancient peoples to Native Americans today.

TALK ABOUT IT

Text Evidence
Draw a box around a sentence that comes from the notes. Why did Amanda include this information in the text?

Grammar
Circle words that give clues about how the text is organized. Why did Amanda organize the text this way?

Condense Ideas
Underline sentences 4 and 5. How can you use the word *and* to combine the sentences to condense the ideas?

Your Turn
Why are some pictographs in danger? Why is it important to take care of the pictographs? Cite text evidence.

» Go Digital!
Write your response online. Use your editing checklist.

TALK ABOUT IT

Weekly Concept Taking a Break

? Essential Question
Why is taking a break important?

>> *Go Digital*

 **What have the friends been doing? Why are they sitting on the bleachers now? What do they still have to do? Write your answers in the chart.**

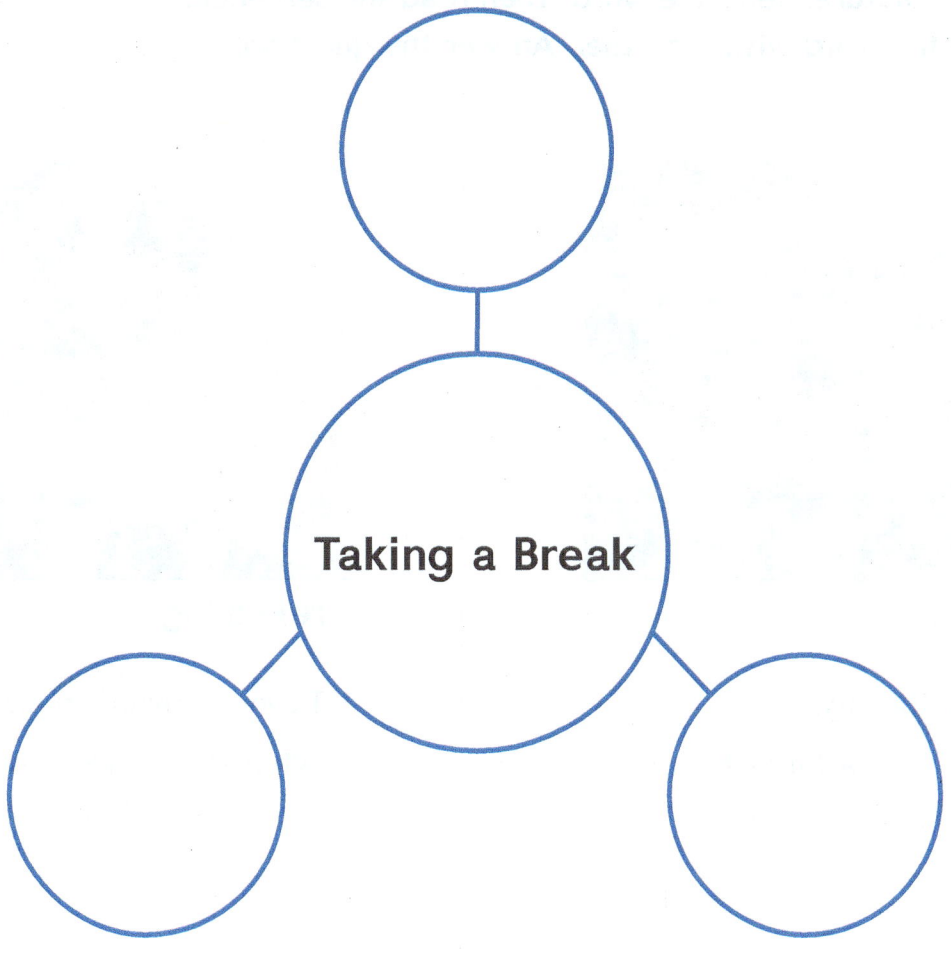

Discuss why it is important to take a break. Use words from the chart. You can say:

The friends have been _____. Now they want to

_____. This will help them finish their _____.

More Vocabulary

 Look at the picture. Read the word. Then read the sentence. Talk about the word with a partner. Answer the question.

lashing

A hurricane is **lashing** the city.

What have you seen rain lashing? How did it look?

_____

_____

_____

revealing

Trevor is **revealing** his birthday present.

What do you like revealing about your favorite TV shows?

_____

_____

_____

Poetry Terms

imagery

Imagery is words that help readers feel, taste, smell, see, or hear something.

The *sweet* and *juicy* watermelon was *cold* and *wet* in her mouth.

repetition

Repetition is the use of the same words or sounds more than once. Poets use repetition to emphasize something.

Kind hearts *are* gardens,
Kind thoughts *are* roots,
Kind words *are* blossoms,
Kind deeds *are* fruits.

hyperbole

Hyperbole is unrealistic language that you are not supposed to believe. It emphasizes a point.

Her *smile is a mile wide*.

COLLABORATE

Work with a partner. Choose the word that creates hyperbole in each sentence. Read each sentence together.

million   mountain   wind

He ate a _____ of carrots.

She ran faster than the _____.

The room was decorated with a _____ flowers.

Text Evidence

1. Talk About It

Read the first stanza. How does the poet feel about the wind?

The poet feels that the wind brings

_____

2. Literary Element
Imagery

Read the second stanza. What images does the poet use to create pictures in your mind about the wind? Underline these images.

3. Specific Vocabulary

Read the last line. The word *roaring* means "growling loudly." What is the poet describing by using the word *roaring*?

The poet is describing how the

wind _____.

Shared Read | Genre • Poetry

An Ode to the Wind

Ode to the wild and whistling wind,
To its power,
To its pleasures,
To the sky that it clears
And the comfort that it brings,
Revealing a warm and radiant sun.

Ode to the wind's uproar,
To its chaos and pandemonium
Unfettered by mountains and mammoth peaks,
Moving deserts and dust great distances,
Whipping snow into undisciplined drifts,
Lashing waves upon dark sand,
Driving flames through bush and bark,
Hissing and roaring like a dragon.

Essential Question

Why is taking a break important?

Read how the poet views opportunities to relax.

Ode to the wind's energy and titanic strength,
Scattering seeds as valuable as gold upon the land,
Filling square-rigged sails with billowing force,
Thrusting ships toward new horizons,
Whipping windmills to turn and generate,
Dispersing autumn leaves to replenish the earth,
To the storms it brings upon us
And the life-giving rain.

Ode to the moving air,
To the warm air rising
And the cool air that comes in to take its place,
To the sky that it cleared
And the comfort it brought,
Rustling hair, cooling fevered brows.
Wind a thousand times softer than silk
Offering a sweet incentive for recreation,
Lifting kites to the outer edge of the stratosphere.

—Jonathan Moss

Make Connections

Talk about how the poet uses images of the wind to make you think about ways to rest and play.
ESSENTIAL QUESTION

How might a windy day help when you need to take a break?
TEXT TO SELF

Text Evidence

❶ Talk About It

Read the third stanza. How does the wind help the land?

The wind helps the land by _____

_____.

❷ Literary Element
Repetition

Read the last stanza. What phrase does the poet repeat at the beginning of every stanza?

The poet repeats the phrase

_____.

❸ Comprehension
Theme

Reread the last stanza. Which images connect a windy day with resting or taking a break? Underline these images.

Respond to the Text

Partner Discussion Work with a partner. Read the questions about "An Ode to the Wind." Show where you found text evidence. Write the page numbers. Then discuss what you learned.

How does the poet connect wind with relaxation?

The poet says the wind brings _____. Page(s): _____

It reveals _____. Page(s): _____

The author describes the wind as softer than _____. Page(s): _____

Text Evidence

What does the poet say about taking a break?

The poet says a windy day is incentive for _____. Page(s): _____

The wind lifts _____. Page(s): _____

So the poet connects wind with _____. Page(s): _____

Text Evidence

Group Discussion Present your answers to the group. Cite text evidence for your ideas. Listen to and discuss the group's opinions.

Write Work with a partner. Look at your notes about "An Ode to the Wind." Write your answer to the Essential Question. Use text evidence to support your answer. Use vocabulary words in your writing.

> **What does the poet say about taking a break?**
>
> The poet says the wind brings _____.
>
> A windy day is incentive for _____.
>
> I think this means _____.

Share Writing Present your writing to the class. Discuss their opinions. Talk about their ideas. Explain why you agree or disagree with their ideas. You can say:

I agree with _____.

That's a good comment, but _____.

Write to Sources

Russell

Take Notes About the Text I took notes on the idea web to answer the question: *How does the poet of "An Ode to the Wind" use strong details to describe the wind?*

pages 56–57

Topic
Strong Details in "An Ode to the Wind"

Detail
"Whipping snow into undisciplined drifts"

Detail
"Driving flames through bush and bark"

Detail
"Hissing and roaring like a dragon"

Detail
"Wind a thousand times softer than silk"

Write About the Text I used notes from my idea web to write an informative text about strong details in "An Ode to the Wind."

Student Model: *Informative Text*

  Jonathan Moss, the poet of "An Ode to the Wind," uses strong details to help readers imagine the wind. Moss writes that the wind can spread flames. When it does this, the wind is "hissing and roaring like a dragon." This detail helps the reader picture a dangerous fire spreading in the wind. Moss also writes that the wind can feel "a thousand times softer than silk." The use of the word *softer* helps the reader imagine how the wind feels. The use of the word *silk* also helps the reader imagine how the wind feels. These details help the reader imagine the wind as both fierce and gentle.

TALK ABOUT IT

Text Evidence
Draw a box around details from the notes that Russell used in his informative text. Why did Russell use these details?

Grammar
Circle the adjectives *fierce* and *gentle* in the last sentence. How are these words related?

Condense Ideas
Underline sentences 6 and 7. How can you combine the sentences to condense the ideas?

Your Turn

Write an informative text about the use of repetition in "An Ode to the Wind."

>> *Go Digital!*
Write your response online. Use your editing checklist.